SPORTS HALL OF ~~FAME~~ WEIRD

KEVIN SYLVESTER

KIDS CAN PRESS

Kids Can Press acknowledges the financial support of the Government of Ontario, through the Ontario Media Development Corporation's Ontario Book Initiative; the Ontario Arts Council; the Canada Council for the Arts; and the Government of Canada, through the BPIDP, for our publishing activity.

Published in Canada by
Kids Can Press Ltd.
29 Birch Avenue
Toronto, ON M4V 1E2

Published in the U.S. by
Kids Can Press Ltd.
2250 Military Road
Tonawanda, NY 14150

www.kidscanpress.com

Edited by Charis Wahl and Shana Hayes
Designed by Julia Naimska

Printed and bound in Canada

CM PA 05 0 9 8 7 6 5 4 3 2 1

National Library of Canada Cataloguing in Publication Data

Sylvester, Kevin
Sports hall of weird / Kevin Sylvester.

ISBN 1-55337-635-8

1. Sports — Miscellanea — Juvenile literature. I. Title.
GV707.S94 2005   j796   C2004-903285-2

Kids Can Press is a *l☺rus*™ Entertainment company

To my great family — Lovely wife, Laura, Excellent Erin, Energetic Emily and our departed cat Drip.

And thanks to the greatest trio of editors in the biz, Liz, Charis and Shana, for all their help in getting this book out of my brain and onto paper.

COME ON IN

Have you ever gone on a field trip to a museum? You wander around looking at stuffed birds, paintings and movies about volcanoes.

This book is kind of like a trip to a museum. A museum of some of the oddest, weirdest and funniest moments in the history of sports.

For example …

We'll visit the Hall of Fowl Balls, where baseball players kill birds and hockey players kill bats. (Yes, there are stuffed birds in this museum, too.)

There's the Hall of Wacky Weather, where they play hockey games no one can see because of the fog — the fog *inside* the arena.

And how about the Hall of Mischievous Mascots, where guys in furry suits wind up in jail.

Are you ready?

Line up for your tickets, get your guidebooks ready, stay with your partner and don't get lost!

Our first stop? — the bathroom.

THE HALL OF URINALS

Did everyone go potty before we started?

If not, here's your chance.

At every major sporting event you'll notice that the lineups for the bathrooms can be incredibly long.

Not everyone can cross their legs for hours, so sometimes there are accidents.

Here are a few.

That doesn't smell like pine tar

Moises Alou is one of the few baseball players who don't wear batting gloves. Gloves can protect your hands from the shock of hitting a 160 km/h (100 mph) fastball.

Alou uses a more unorthodox method to help his hands cope.

He pees on them.

It works, somehow. Alou has been one of baseball's best hitters for years.

But you may notice his teammates refusing the traditional post–home run handshake.

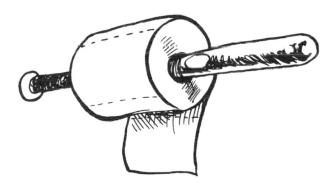

Urine my way!

Not all ball players use urinals for their intended purpose.

Baseball great George Brett once used a urinal for batting practice.

During a particularly bad hitting slump, Brett stormed into a locker room in Minnesota, grabbed a bat and took out his frustration on a helpless urinal.

Then a toilet.

Then a sink.

A few bent pipes and porcelain shards later, Brett was still in a hitting slump (too bad they don't pitch urinals).

When you gotta go, you gotta go

British soccer player Robbie Savage once had a bathroom visit cost him thousands of dollars.

Savage was taking medication for an injured leg, but the medicine made him feel sick.

At one game he felt sure he was going to hurl. He dashed into his team's locker room, but both of the toilets were in use. So he ran to the nearest bathroom he could find.

It was the toilet in the referee's locker room and Savage used it — just in time.

But there are strict rules about players and officials being separate at all times. British soccer officials fined Savage two weeks' pay, or more than $100 000, for "improper conduct."

That's an expensive puke!

My ticket says that's MY toilet

One lacrosse team made their toilets the best seats in the house.

The Philadelphia Wings said they wanted to treat their fans like royalty. And what does royalty sit on? A throne. (Throne is a slang term for a toilet.)

The fans thought the idea was hilarious.

At every game, two lucky fans got the chance to sit at rink level, on toilets. They were given crowns, free food and plungers as their scepters.

The team had two simple rules for the fans: don't actually *use* the toilets, and put the seat down at the end of the game.

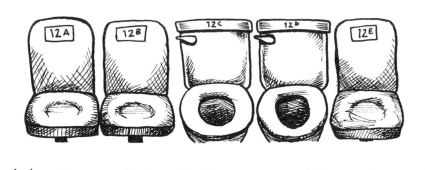

Smells like a winner

No story could be weirder than the one about the competitions that were held in ancient Japan.

Towns would often gather together their champions for major tournaments — for farting.

Prizes and admiring smiles from their townsfolk would go to the loudest and longest flatulators.

Now everyone hold your nose until we get to our next stop.

FOWL BALLS!

A mangled menagerie.

It's amazing how many animals have croaked so that athletes could enjoy their games.

Footballs are called "pigskins."

Baseballs are made from cowhide, and badminton players smash "birdies."

Sometimes athletes smash real birdies as well.

Down under

Michael Llodra and Julien Boutter were playing against each other in a doubles tennis match at the Australian Open.

A bird flew across the court, chasing a moth it wanted for dinner. Just as Llodra hit the ball, the bird swooped over the net.

The ball hit the bird and killed it instantly.

Boutter ran over to the body and said a quick prayer. But he realized the bird would not recover so he kneeled over it and performed the last rights. The other players joined in the impromptu funeral ceremony.

The bird was carried away and the players resumed their match.

The incident didn't phase Llodra. He and his partner won the match.

Llodra said afterward he didn't mean to hit the bird, but at least he saved the moth.

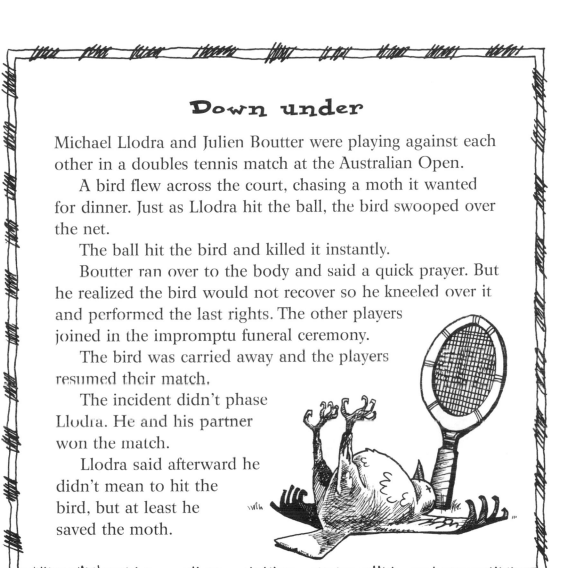

The bird just went poof

Arizona pitcher Randy Johnson can throw the ball over 160 km/h (100 mph) — that's fast!

Johnson threw one of these pitches during a game just as a dove flew over home plate.

Ball and bird arrived at exactly the same moment and there was an explosion of feathers.

I didn't sea that gull!

During a game, baseball player Dave Winfield threw the ball high up in the air. It hit a seagull, which fell down to the field, dead.

Toronto police charged Winfield with cruelty to animals.

Winfield claimed it was an accident. His manager told the police that Winfield couldn't have done it on purpose because he couldn't throw accurately enough.

Maybe the insult worked. The police dropped the charges.

Bats about hockey

During the 1975 Stanley Cup finals, a bat snuck into the hockey rink. The bat swooped down on the fans and players.

One player, Jim Lorentz, decided he'd had enough.

Lorentz waited for the bat to fly close to him, then he lifted his stick and whacked it out of the air.

Another player calmly picked up the lifeless bat and carried it off the ice. But Lorentz was forever known as "Batman."

Anyone want a bird-sicle?

The Pittsburgh Penguins thought they had the perfect mascot for their first NHL season.

A real penguin named Slapshot Pete.

Pete would ride on the Zamboni® ice resurfacer between periods.

But the show didn't last long.

The bird had been born in a zoo and had never been on ice or out in the cold.

Pete soon died — of pneumonia.

Let's play FLING THE FISH!

Hockey fans in Detroit have a long tradition of flinging an octopus onto the ice for good luck.

The tradition was started in 1952 by local fish merchants Pete and Jerry Cusimano. In those days, it took eight wins to claim the Stanley Cup.

Eight wins, eight legs.

They grabbed an octopus from the shop, smuggled it into the rink and threw it on the ice.

The Detroit Red Wings did win the Stanley Cup that year, and a really gross tradition was born.

NATURE FIGHTS BACK

You might find a stuffed athlete in this room.
  Our next stop shows us how animals
fight back.
  Tricky crows, hungry rats and enough
moths to clog your lungs.

Throw another moth on the bar-b-q

Sydney, Australia, hosted the 2000 Summer Olympic Games. Thousands of athletes showed up. So did hundreds of thousands of Bogong moths. They are some of the biggest moths in the world. They are about the size of your hand.

At one point organizers even handed out "moth swatters" to help the crowds deal with the flying pests.

Athletes were bugged by them as well. One runner started a race too early because a moth landed on her foot.

Finally organizers figured out that if they turned off the stadium lights at night the moths would just go away.

That's not the kind of birdie I wanted

One sport that seems to be plagued by animal interference is golf.

Some golfers in Ohio would hit great shots, but when they'd walk to where their balls should have been, the balls were gone.

It turned out that a hungry crow was entranced by the lovely, round, white bobbles.

He'd swoop down on a ball, snatch it in his beak and carry it off to his nest.

Another bad birdie

A crow in West Virigina made a different kind of name for himself.

He would wait until the golfers got out of their carts to shoot their balls.

Then he would swoop down and steal their snacks.

That pooch didn't like my smooch

The pooch in question belonged to David Cone's mother. Cone was one of the New York Yankees' best pitchers. One day he was visiting his mother and he reached out his hand to pet her Jack Russell terrier.

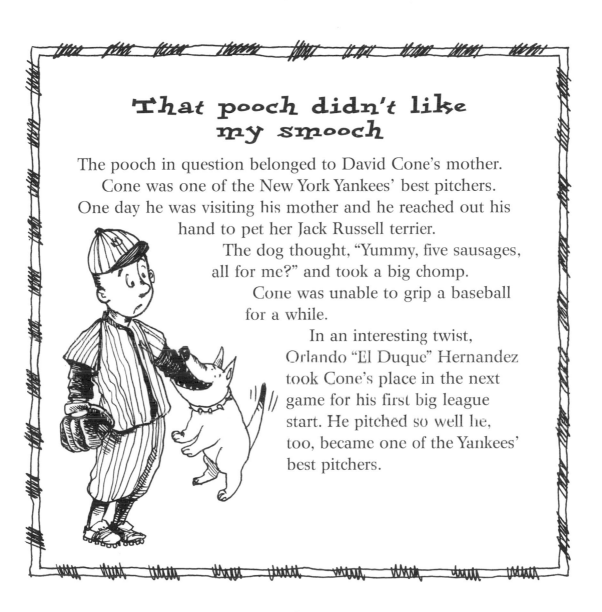

The dog thought, "Yummy, five sausages, all for me?" and took a big chomp.

Cone was unable to grip a baseball for a while.

In an interesting twist, Orlando "El Duque" Hernandez took Cone's place in the next game for his first big league start. He pitched so well he, too, became one of the Yankees' best pitchers.

One foxy thief

Foxes are known as crafty animals, and one fox in Sweden almost ruined a golf tournament.

The fox would sneak out onto the course and steal as many balls as it could get.

It was apparently collecting food for the winter and thought the golf balls were bird eggs. (Imagine the fox's disappointment when it actually bit one.)

Golfers were worried they'd lose strokes for each ball the fox stole. Tournament organizers eventually allowed the golfers to just play another ball — with no penalty strokes.

Baseball rats

Rats haunt almost every sporting site, eating leftover food that sloppy sports fans leave behind after each game. Usually there are enough leftovers to feed many rats.

How many rats?

Well, a few years ago the folks in Seattle decided to build a new stadium.

So they blew up the old one.

As soon as the explosion started, thousands of rats came streaming out of the rubble.

TV, LAUNDRY AND BEING OUTSIDE ARE DANGEROUS

Some of the weirdest injuries happen in sports.

You could call this a visit to the Hospital Wing of our sports museum.

Athletes rely on their bodies to keep them competing for as long as possible. And they try to take very good care of themselves.

But injuries are a constant danger. It's amazing how little it can take to wreck a knee or an ankle or a wrist.

All I did was change the channel!

Didn't your mother ever tell you too much TV is bad for you?

English soccer superstar Rio Ferdinand was relaxing the night before a big match. He decided the best way to keep his mind off the game was to put his legs up, stretch out and watch some TV.

He did — for a long time.

When he decided it was time to turn off the TV, he got up. But his knee suddenly shot with pain. He'd stayed in the same position for so long his leg locked up on him.

Ferdinand missed the big game (and a couple after that), but presumably he watched them on TV.

Where did *that* wall come from?

You sometimes hear baseball commentators remark that a player "went right to the wall" to make an amazing catch.

Rodney McCray did them all one better. He went right *through* the wall.

He was playing outfield when the batter hit a long fly ball. The ball was going over McCray's head, so he charged straight back to track it down. He never took his eye off it. Which is why he didn't see the outfield wall approaching fast.

McCray never slowed down as he crashed into the wall, knocking a hole right through it.

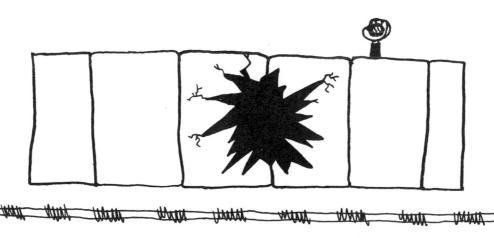

He died of a broken heart

One of the most tragic stories in sports is that of Howie Morenz. He was a star player with the Montreal Canadiens in the 1930s.

In 1937, Morenz crashed into the boards and broke his leg in three places. The doctors told him he would recover, but he would never be strong enough to play hockey again.

Morenz died two days later. His friends and teammates said he'd died of a broken heart.

Fifteen thousand fans attended his funeral at the Montreal Forum, home of the Canadiens.

It's only a flesh wound

Soccer goalie Bert Trautman once won a championship with a broken neck.

He was the keep for Manchester City back in the 1956 championship game.

During the game he took a hard shot off his head and noticed his neck felt a little stiff. But he shrugged it off and kept playing. He made save after save and his team won the game 3–1 over Birmingham City.

Then Trautman really noticed his neck throbbing with pain. He'd actually played the second half of the game with a broken neck.

At least it wasn't his underwear

Atlanta pitcher John Smoltz showed up for training practice with a huge burn on his chest.

He'd burned *himself*! Smoltz had tried to iron out a wrinkly shirt — while he was still wearing it.

When his teammates made fun of him, Smoltz responded by saying that'd he'd done the same thing a number of times without burning himself.

Good thing he wasn't wearing wrinkly pants.

Hey, can you run over my pants, too?

Ryan Smyth wanted nothing more than to grow up to be a hockey player.

One year his hometown hosted a training camp for some of the top players in the world.

Smyth was so excited. Especially when he saw Edmonton player Glenn Anderson getting into his car. Smyth ran across the parking lot to get Anderson's

autograph, or at least to say "hi."

Unfortunately, Anderson didn't see Smyth coming, and he got into his car and backed up over him.

Smyth wasn't hurt (who says hockey players aren't tough?), but he did have a big skid mark across the shirt he was wearing.

Smyth refused to clean the shirt.

CRAZY FANS

Now we should stop to pay attention to the people who watch sporting events.
What would sports be without the fans?
Actually, it would just be a bunch of jocks running around a lot.

Three blind mice

Organ music has been wafting out of baseball parks for years.

But one famous organist in Clearwater, Florida, made an unfortunate selection.

During a game in 1985 the umpire made a call against the home team. Organist Wilbur Snapp wasn't impressed. He immediately broke out with a version of "Three Blind Mice."

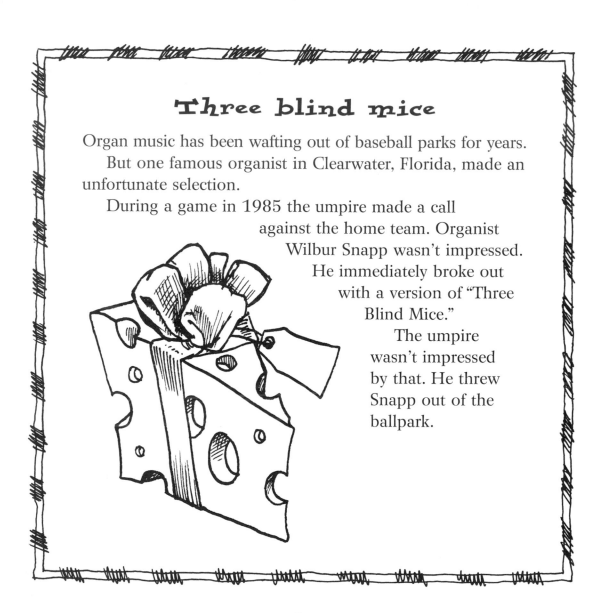

The umpire wasn't impressed by that. He threw Snapp out of the ballpark.

Why does that nun have a beard?

One of the craziest fans in sports is Jerry Marlowe.

He's a huge fan of the Ohio State Buckeyes. And he's taken in their annual football game against Michigan for twenty straight years — without ever buying a ticket.

Marlowe sneaks into games in disguise.

He has dressed as a referee, a cheerleader, a concession stand worker and even once as a nun.

I guess sneaking into sports events is a "bad habit."

Soccer to 'im

Soccer fans are the craziest. When a game is on they notice nothing else.

Guards at a prison in Jakarta were so intent on watching every second of the 2002 World Cup match between Brazil and Belgium they didn't notice some inmates escaping.

You might understand if it had been just two or three inmates escaping. But by the time the guards noticed what was going on, forty-eight inmates had walked away.

The Klongprem Prison in Bangkok came up with a solution for soccer mania.

The inmates were split into teams and competed for a mock World Cup.

Prisoners were also allowed to watch the real games on TV.

No one tried to escape.

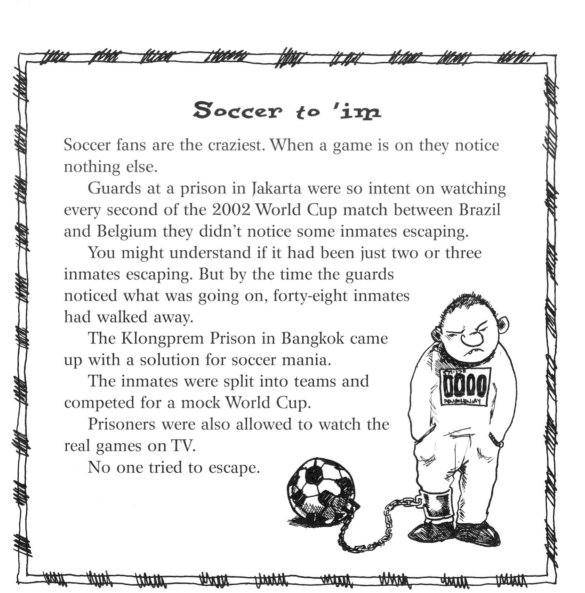

The church of soccer

Soccer can even come before higher pursuits.

The Anglican Church was worried no one would show up for church during the 2002 World Cup. So a number of parishes held their services earlier, then put TV screens on their altars or lawns.

One put a sign out front reading "Make Jesus the Center Forward of Your Life" and urged the fans to come to church in their England jerseys.

The temple of soccer

David Beckham is one of the most revered soccer players of all time.

A Buddhist soccer fan in Thailand made a statue of Beckham, covered it with gold leaf and placed it in the Pariwas temple at the feet of the main Buddha statue.

Some visitors to the temple were outraged.

But the senior monk argued that soccer has become a kind of religion and the statue could stay.

This doesn't look like Spain

Sometimes soccer fans will travel halfway around the world to watch their favorite team.

Two fans from England didn't want to go that far, but did anyway.

They decided to take in a Manchester United game in Spain. They asked for two flights to Santiago. And they got two flights to Santiago.

But not Santiago, Spain — Santiago, Chile.

Even with the extra eleven hours on the plane, they didn't miss the match.

They watched it on TV as soon as they landed.

How much for his underwear?

Sports fans love to collect objects their favorite players have used, touched or, in one case, chewed with.

Ty Cobb was one of the greatest baseball hitters of all time. Late in his life he also lost his teeth. What's the connection?

Well, a few years ago someone decided to buy them.

Yes, Karen Shemonsky paid $8000 for his dentures.

Yes, his dentures! Yes, $8000!

How much for the wrapper?

Arizona's Luis Gonzalez chewed a piece of gum then spit it out during a baseball game. A few days later he was shocked to learn that a fan claimed to have picked up the gum and was auctioning it off — for $10 000.

But how could the fan prove it was the right piece of gum?

Someone suggested that Gonzalez provide a DNA sample. Gonzalez got a little sick of the story, and decided to end it. He chewed another piece of gum, in front of witnesses, then spit it into a container and sent it to the auction winner.

I knew something was wrong when he wasn't wearing a uniform

A football fan once got in trouble for standing in a team's huddle.

Otis Henry ran onto the field in New Orleans. He ran into the visiting team's huddle and asked the players if anyone would like his autograph.

No one did.

But Henry pulled out a pen and tried to write his name on one of their jerseys anyway.

Police eventually nabbed him and charged him with disturbing the peace. Police say he was acting on a dare.

The naked truth

Sometimes fans run on the field naked. They're known as streakers. Usually they streak outdoors, where it's warm.

But one fan stripped at a Calgary Flames hockey game.

His name was Tim Hurlbut, and he was planning to hurl his butt onto the ice surface. He stripped down to his red socks as his fellow fans watched in amazement.

Then he leapt for the glass, red socks blazing, and got caught on the glass, fell on his head and knocked himself out cold.

Hurlbut revived just as medical staff were carrying him off on a stretcher. He raised his arms in celebration.

Police charged him with mischief.

CEMETERY

FANS FROM BEYOND THE GRAVE

Watch out in this next room.

Not all fans stop cheering once they stop breathing. You might sit down for a rest and find out you're on someone's grave!

That kind of bad luck could curse you for years.

Curses are serious. Some sports teams have suffered for years.

Step lightly.

Rest in peace ... or in seat 12A

Paul Wellener was a rabid fan of his hometown football team, the Pittsburgh Steelers.

He was a season ticket holder for forty-two years.

But eventually, all things must end and Wellener said farewell to his family, his world and his team.

Well, actually, not his team.

Wellener's family buried him but didn't put a normal gravestone on top.

They put Wellener's seats over the grave.

Hey it's snowing ... in July?

One fan of the Seattle Mariners asked to have his ashes spread over the team's ballpark.

But he never told the team.

This was in the summer of 2002, and people were very worried about terrorist attacks. During the game, the fans looked up and saw an airplane dropping a package of fine powder over the field.

It wasn't poison, just the man's ashes. But frightened fans bolted from the stadium.

The curse of the goat

The Chicago Cubs haven't won a World Series in more than a hundred years. Many people blame "the goat."

During the 1945 World Series, local tavern owner Billy Sianis brought a goat to the Cubs' home games. He would get the goat to baaah at opposing teams.

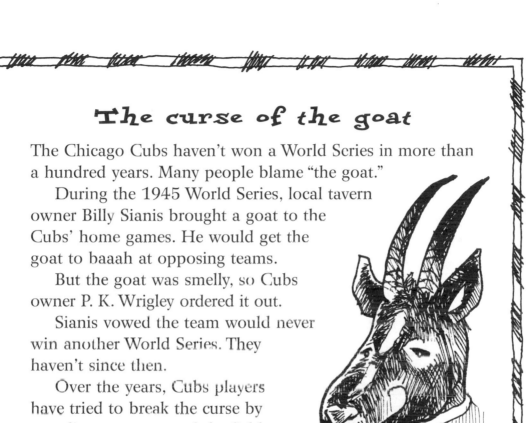

But the goat was smelly, so Cubs owner P. K. Wrigley ordered it out.

Sianis vowed the team would never win another World Series. They haven't since then.

Over the years, Cubs players have tried to break the curse by parading goats around the field. So far, nothing has worked.

The Forum's unseen cheering section

Some ghostly supporters have been credited with changing the outcomes of the games themselves.

For years the Montreal Canadiens of the National Hockey League ruled the sport and won game after game in their home, the Forum.

Opposing players would swear that the ghosts of the team's great players would help the Canadiens by making pucks bounce in odd ways, or tripping up opposing players.

The Canadiens, like many modern teams, left their old arena a few years ago for a newer, bigger rink. They have yet to win a Stanley Cup there.

The curse of the Bambino

Boston Red Sox owner Harry Frazee made one of the biggest mistakes of all time.

He owned the Boston Red Sox when they were the best team in baseball. They won World Series after World Series. And they had the best young player in baseball, Babe "the Bambino" Ruth.

But Frazee also owned a theater and he hadn't put on a hit show in a while.

So in 1919 he did the unthinkable. He sold Babe Ruth to the hated New York Yankees. Frazee used the money to start a series of new plays. One, *No, No, Nanette*, became a hit

Ruth led the Yankees to their first World Series title. The team itself went on to win more than 20 titles.

It took the Red Sox 86 years to win their next World Series. In 2004, they beat the hated New York Yankees to win the division, then they swept St. Louis for the World Series title.

Find the dead guy, win the Cup

The Toronto Maple Leafs won the Stanley Cup in 1951. The winning goal was scored by Bill Barilko. As he was falling to the ice, he shot the puck into the net.

After the final, Barilko went on a fishing trip in Canada's North. His plane crashed, but, mysteriously, searchers could not find his body. They eventually gave up and the Leafs fell on hard times on the ice.

In fact the Leafs didn't win another Cup until 1962 — the season Barilko's body was discovered!

Some believe his ghost refused to let the Leafs win until his body had been recovered.

MISCHIEVOUS MASCOTS

I'm afraid you have to dress up like a chipmunk or a chicken to get a real feel for this next room.

You could call it our Mascot Menagerie. It's unclear where the idea of mascots comes from. Old teams used to have pets with them in games for good luck.

But in the twentieth century someone decided it would be great to have a person dress up like an animal, do silly things and get the crowd more into the games.

Pretty soon every team wanted a wacky cheerleader.

But if they only knew what they were getting themselves into.

This swan is still an ugly duckling

One of the most troublesome mascots is Cyril the Swan.

A swan is a regal creature. Beautiful, graceful, a universal symbol of animal excellence.

Cyril is none of these things.

Cyril is the mascot for the English soccer club Swansea, and he gets into all sorts of trouble.

He's been suspended for throwing food at opposing fans, arguing calls with referees and even getting into a fight with another team's coach.

And a few seasons ago, Cyril ripped the head off an opposing mascot, Zampa the Lion, and kicked it into the crowd. Soccer officials suspended Cyril for two games.

Jailbird

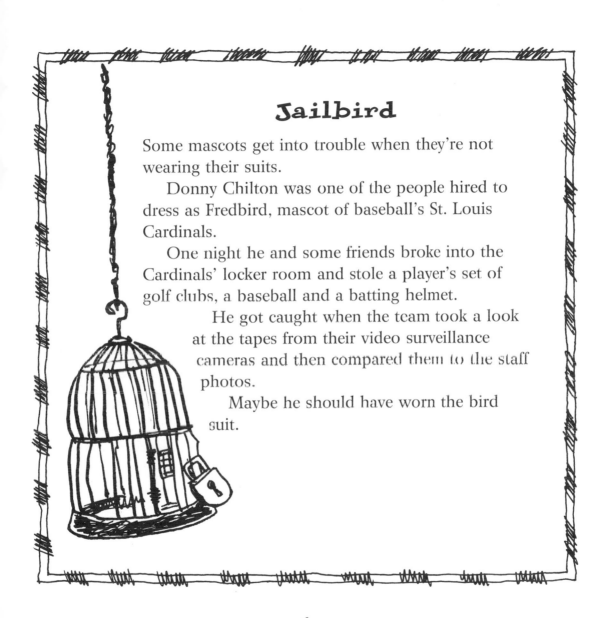

Some mascots get into trouble when they're not wearing their suits.

Donny Chilton was one of the people hired to dress as Fredbird, mascot of baseball's St. Louis Cardinals.

One night he and some friends broke into the Cardinals' locker room and stole a player's set of golf clubs, a baseball and a batting helmet.

He got caught when the team took a look at the tapes from their video surveillance cameras and then compared them to the staff photos.

Maybe he should have worn the bird suit.

He can't bark without his tongue

The Calgary Flames have a mascot named Harvey the Hound.

The Flames were hosting their arch rivals, the Edmonton Oilers, and had a 4–0 lead in the third period of the hockey game. Harvey decided this was the perfect time to taunt the Oilers bench. He leaned over the glass and started mocking Oilers head coach Craig MacTavish.

MacTavish was not amused. He reached up, grabbed Harvey's red felt tongue and ripped it out. He held it up to show the crowd, then threw it into the stands.

Harvey may have lost his tongue but not his voice — he continued to insult the Oilers.

MacTavish grabbed a stick. He was about to use it to attack Harvey when his own team restrained him. The Oilers players started squirting Harvey with their water bottles.

Security finally came over and escorted Harvey to safer ground.

Please stand for the Lord Mayor H'Angus the Monkey

H'Angus the Monkey is the mascot for England's Hartlepool United soccer team.

He's also the Lord Mayor of the city.

Stuart Drummond officially ran for mayor but did so dressed up as his alter ego, H'Angus, the simian soccer supporter.

One of his campaign promises? Schools had recently canceled a program to give the students free milk, so H'Angus vowed to give the children free bananas. He won.

TROPHY TRIALS AND TRIBULATIONS

Make sure you have your sunglasses on.

We're heading into a room full of silver cups, dented plates, even a mounted axe.

Be careful, and don't touch anything.

The athletes have done enough damage without your help.

Ashes to ashes

One of the odder "trophies" in sports isn't a trophy at all. It's a bunch of smelly old ashes.

Given to the winner of cricket matches between England and Australia, the trophy was created back in 1882.

When Australia upset England for the first time, the English papers suggested fans had burned the wickets in mourning for the loss.

The next time England played Australia, someone took up the theme and burned an actual pair of cricket stumps.

The ashes now reside in an urn and have spent most of the recent years in Australia.

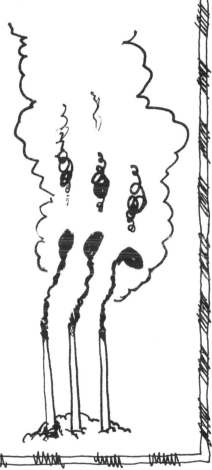

Every dent tells a story

Hockey's Stanley Cup is probably the most loved and most mistreated trophy of all time. It's been lost, dented and stolen.

There was the time Ottawa's Harry Smith kicked the Cup into the Rideau Canal.

Smith had a little too much to drink at a party and decided to see how far he could drop-kick the trophy.

It wasn't until the next day that he realized what he'd done. He ran back to the canal.

Miraculously, the Cup was still there, dented, but not lost.

The Canadian Football League's Grey Cup has been through a lot, too.

Once, the Edmonton Eskimos returned the Cup to the league in pieces — a player had sat on it during a wild victory party.

A couple of years later another Eskimo player head-butted the Cup and knocked the top off.

Kick the ball, not the trophy!

Soccer's World Cup trophy has had an incredible history of misfortune.

During the Second World War, head soccer honcho Ottorino Barassi hid it under his bed in a shoe box to keep it from the Nazis.

In 1966, the trophy was on display in London when it was stolen. Police spent a week looking for it and came up empty. A dog named Pickles spotted it hidden in a hedge.

The last time it was stolen, in 1983, was the last time it was ever seen.

Brazil had put the trophy on display. But masked robbers broke into the Brazilian soccer federation and stole the Cup. Before police could catch the thieves, they had melted it down for its gold.

Give 'em the Axe

Cal State and Stanford play a football game for the Axe every year.

The game that started it all was in 1899.

Stanford fans were using an axe to chop up gold and blue ribbons — Cal's school colors.

The Cal fans didn't like that one bit so they stole the axe and threatened to use it to chop more than ribbons.

Tempers eventually settled and officials from both schools agreed that the axe would go to the winner of their annual football game.

EXTREME SPORTS OR EXTREME STUPIDITY?

Ignore the screaming coming from the next room.

It's the parents of the athletes, watching their kids dive without oxygen, sail around the world alone and literally lose their heads.

Some of these sports are designed to be extreme.

Others just end up being extreme.

See you on my fifteenth birthday ... I hope

Fourteen-year-old Subaru Takahashi of Japan set sail alone on a windy afternoon in the summer of 1996.

He had a two-month supply of food and water on board and was planning on sailing nonstop across the Pacific Ocean from Japan to San Francisco.

He almost didn't make it.

First, his radio died.

Then his navigation equipment died.

Then his parents assumed he'd died.

But on September 13, a month late, he appeared like a ghost ship out of the fog and sailed into San Francisco Bay.

He was the youngest person to make the trip safely.

No tank? No thanks

The goal of extreme diving is to submerge a diver under water as deep as possible without an oxygen tank.

Divers are dropped into the water, dragged down, given one breath from an oxygen tank, then told to rise to the surface.

Frenchman Loïc Leferme has set the world record a number of times. One of those dives he was under water for three and a half minutes and dropped to 162 meters (530 ft.) below sea level.

The divers hope to make it back up alive.

Leferme did.

Not all do.

Just a week before Leferme's record dive, Audrey Mestre, another French diver, died while trying to go 170 meters (558 ft.) under the sea.

Across the moss playing lacrosse

Lacrosse was played by North America's native peoples long before the Europeans showed up.

The games would sometimes travel over miles and miles. And the games could be violent. More than once a player died from head injuries suffered when an opposing player cracked him over the skull.

But dying was about the only thing that could keep a player out of the game. Quitting because of an open wound or broken bone was frowned upon.

You lose the game, and your head

The Aztecs of ancient Mexico had the toughest game. It was called *ollamaliztli*.

The game was played in an enclosed stone arena. Players would be split into two teams. A hole was carved out of the middle of one wall and both teams would try to maneuver to the hole and kick the ball through.

That doesn't sound too extreme.

What was extreme was what happened if you lost.

You were killed.

The game was part sport, part religious service, and the losing team was sacrificed to the gods. They were sacrificed by having their insides removed while they were still alive.

Have a cup of tea —
We could be here a while

Cricket is one of the slowest games ever invented. Matches can stretch on for days.

It's the only sport with tea breaks built in, just to let the players refresh and recharge.

But one cricket match went on a little too long.

In the 1920s, England was playing a game against the West Indies. The game continued on and on and was still undecided eight days later.

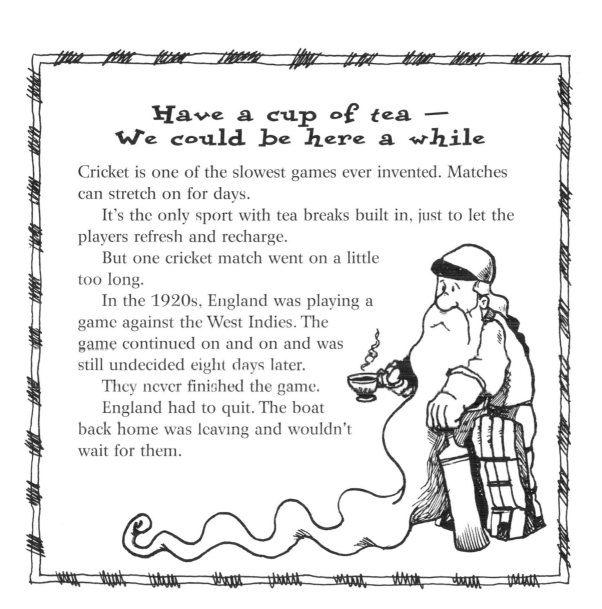

They never finished the game.

England had to quit. The boat back home was leaving and wouldn't wait for them.

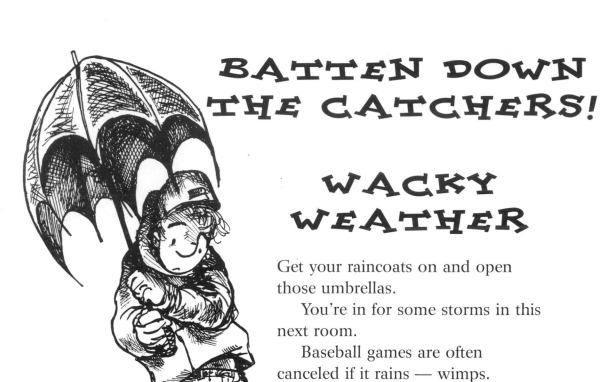

BATTEN DOWN THE CATCHERS!

WACKY WEATHER

Get your raincoats on and open those umbrellas.

You're in for some storms in this next room.

Baseball games are often canceled if it rains — wimps.

I mist the football

Fog once split a football game in two.

The game was the final of the Canadian Football League season in 1962.

The Winnipeg Bluebombers and Hamilton Tiger-Cats were meeting for the Grey Cup. They started the game on the afternoon of December 1. There was a little fog at first, but not enough to delay the game.

The fog kept rolling in off the lake, and by the fourth quarter you couldn't see anything. So officials rescheduled the final ten minutes to the following day.

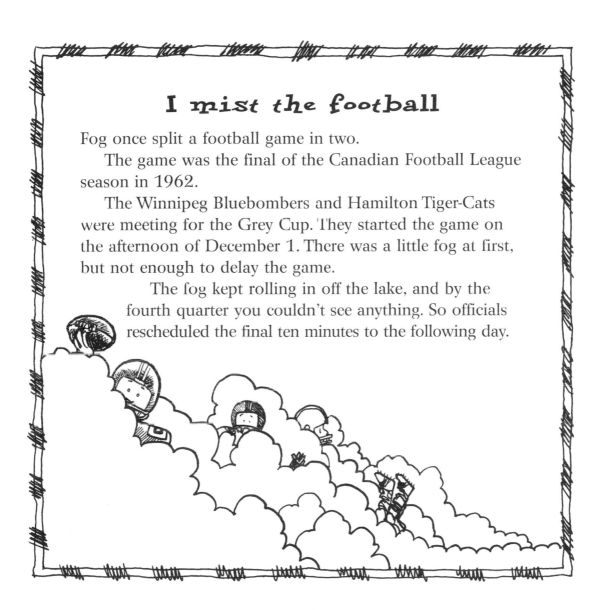

I mist the puck

The Buffalo Sabres were hosting the Philadelphia Flyers in game three of the Stanley Cup finals in 1975.

It was cold on the ice, but hot and humid outside. That combination creates fog.

The referees asked the players to skate around in circles to help break the fog up. It helped a little, but the players could still only see a few feet ahead.

The referees had to stop the game a number of times to get the players to skate around. Each time the ice would clear just enough to resume play.

Buffalo goaltender Gerry Desjardins quit after two periods because he couldn't see anything.

They eventually finished the game, and Buffalo won it 5–4 in overtime.

One weird win

A newspaper in Kinshasa, Congo, reported one bizarre accident. According to the story, lightning struck at a soccer game in the east of the country with unbelievable results.

The lightning killed only the visiting team.

The home team received minor burns.

Fans were convinced someone had cursed the visitors.

It's winter inside

When the weather doesn't cooperate, you sometimes have to make your own.

Japan has some of the best ski hills in the world, but not enough to satisfy the country's desire for the slopes.

So some smart businessmen in Tokyo came up with a solution.

They built a mountain downtown.

But it doesn't snow enough in Tokyo so they built the mountain indoors. And they use snowmaking machines to keep it winter all year long.

GOOD GUYS FINISH LAST

You might want to enter this room after everyone else. That's how the people in the room got there. You could call it the Hall of Lovable Losers.

Football coach Vince Lombardi once said "Good guys finish last."

This chapter, then, must be full of some of the greatest guys of all time. Because they all finished last.

Stop horsing around

If you have ever watched a horse race, you'll know that there are favorites and longshots.

Favorites are expected to win. Longshots probably won't, but could.

And then there are two horses in a category all their own. Quixall Crossett and Zippy Chippy were "noshots."

Quixall Crossett holds the all-time record — 103 races, 103 losses. He even had a race named after him late in his career, and lost that one, too.

Zippy Chippy only lost all 90 or so races he started.

But he's special because one race wasn't even against other horses. In 2000, Zippy Chippy raced baseball player Jose Herrera.

They lined up for a 36 meter (40 yd.) dash.

Herrera won.

Maybe you should try another sport

Eddie the Eagle competed for England at the Winter Olympics in 1988 in Calgary.

As a ski jumper.

England has no real snowy winter and no ski jumping hills. Eddie practiced by jumping into a swimming pool.

The crowds in Calgary cheered Eddie, but also hoped he wouldn't kill himself. Eddie was able to land, barely. His jumps put him firmly in last place, but he smiled through the whole experience and became one of the most popular athletes of the 1988 games.

Who's the worst?

The best soccer countries in the world compete in the World Cup.

One year the worst soccer countries staged a tournament of their own.

In 2002 those countries were Bhutan and Montserrat. While the World Cup was taking place in Asia that year, the players from these two countries got together for the "Other World Cup final."

The winner wouldn't get much, but the loser would be saddled with the tag "worst soccer country in the world."

Bhutan won the game, 4–0.

I'll take the dead guy

Footballer Garney Henley made two mistakes while heading up the Ottawa Rough Riders as general manager.

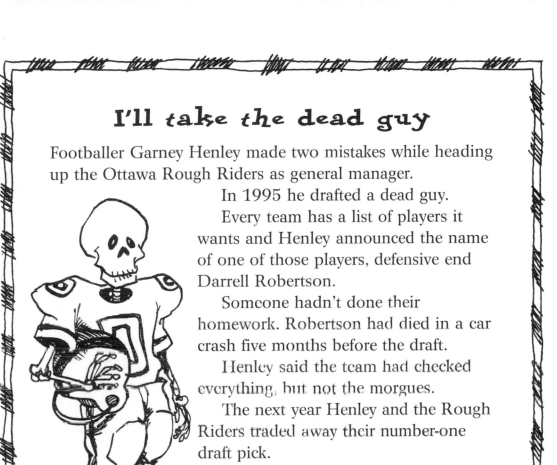

In 1995 he drafted a dead guy.

Every team has a list of players it wants and Henley announced the name of one of those players, defensive end Darrell Robertson.

Someone hadn't done their homework. Robertson had died in a car crash five months before the draft.

Henley said the team had checked everything, but not the morgues.

The next year Henley and the Rough Riders traded away their number-one draft pick.

That's not unusual. What was unusual was that they'd traded the pick to two different teams.

YOU ARE WHAT YOU EAT ... GROSS

You might want to grab some lunch before you hit this next room.

You may not want to eat afterward, unless green cheese steaks, stale tuna and bad hamburger are your faves.

Next time I'll bring my own

The Detroit Red Wings hockey team was on a flight back home when dinner was served.

Most of the players had the Philly Cheese Steak and Coleslaw. Yum-yum.

The next day the team was getting ready to play St. Louis when the players who'd had the cheese steak started getting sick. Yup, food poisoning.

Luckily for the team, not all the Red Wings had had that meal.

Henrik Zetterberg had said he wasn't hungry and just munched on some fruit. He was healthy enough to play and scored the game-winning goal in overtime as Detroit beat St. Louis 4–3.

I'll stick to kiwifruit

The New Zealand rugby team once blamed food poisoning for losing the World Cup.

They were playing South Africa in South Africa.

The night before the big match the team ate together in their hotel. They thought the waitress looked suspicious, but they ate their meal anyway.

The next day they all felt sick.

South Africa won the title. The New Zealand team said they'd been posioned.

The next time around they brought their own cooks.

Get your hot dogs here!

The food vendors at soccer's 2002 World Cup of Soccer were extremely happy when the fans from around the world started showing up for the games.

They even launched a series of stands to sell one of the local favorites — dog meat.

World Cup organizers shut them down. They said it would give the world a bad image of local cuisine.

Sumo size that for me

The biggest eaters in sports are sumo wrestlers. They weigh in at around 180 kg (400 lb.) each.

The goal of the sport is to knock an opposing sumo out of a ring that's marked on the ground.

Often, the fatter wrestlers are, the better they do.

Wrestlers will exercise in the morning, then sit down for a big meal of *chanko-nabe* stew (made of tofu, veggies and meat) and bowls and bowls of rice.

Then they sleep — for hours.

The rest helps the food turn into fat.

GET YOUR TICKETS HERE

If you don't have your tickets already, you can get some here.

But be prepared to pay through the nose.

This room puts the scalp in scalping.

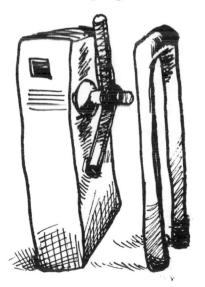

If you hadn't moved, the ball would have missed you

Alice Roth was watching a baseball game in Philadelphia. Phillies' star Richie Ashburn was at the plate. He fouled off a pitch that smacked Roth right in the face and broke her nose.

The game was halted for a few moments as the stadium staff ran over to make sure she was okay. The game resumed while they were getting ready to help Roth to the hospital.

Ashburn was still at bat, and he fouled off the next pitch as well.

Guess who that ball hit?

Yup, Alice Roth, as she was being carried off on a stretcher.

Stand up or get out

The University of Florida Gators football team prides itself on working hard every moment.

In fact, they have a rule that no player is allowed to sit during a practice — the policy extends to the fans as well.

One fan showed up to watch the Gators' first practice and had a seat in the stands.

Security staff politely talked to him and asked him to stand. He refused, so they kicked him out.

Fore! I mean
FOOOOOOOOOOOORD

Former U.S. President Gerald Ford was an avid golfer —
if not a great one.

Ford was so notorious for hitting spectators
with golf balls that comedian Bob Hope once
joked, "It's not hard to find Jerry Ford on a golf
course — you just follow the wounded."

Ford played along as well, saying "I know I'm
getting better at golf because I'm hitting fewer
spectators."

Excuse me ma'am, but could you hold still?

Hale Irwin hit one of the strangest shots in golf at a tournament in 1973.

The ball flew through the air and landed in the crowd.

Irwin went to look for it, but for the life of him, he couldn't see the ball anywhere.

Then a woman in the crowd tapped him on the shoulder. Amazingly the ball had come down and landed in her bra.

The rules state you have to hit the ball where it lands or else retrieve it yourself and take a penalty. The first option could have been painful, and the second was just plain embarrassing.

Tournament organizers ruled Irwin could drop the ball without a penalty. And that the woman could retrieve the ball for Irwin, again without a penalty.

NOT SO PEARLY GATES

GREAT SWINDLES AND CHEATS

You might have to sneak into this next room.

It's full of people who sneaked their way to fame and fortune and, sometimes, failure.

It's amazing what some people will do to finish first.

Harding har har

Figure skater Tonya Harding was involved in a real struggle with arch rival Nancy Kerrigan. Both were considered favorites for the U.S. championship, but only one could win.

The weekend of the big tournament finally came. After one of the practices, a cloaked figure smashed Kerrigan across the leg with a metal pipe. Kerrigan fell over in pain and couldn't compete.

Harding went on to win the championship and earn herself a spot at the Olympic Games.

But before long the story came out. The Harding team had hired a hit man to break Kerrigan's legs. Her husband had made the payment. Kerrigan demanded that Harding be kicked out of the Olympics.

Both eventually competed. Kerrigan finished second. Harding, perhaps thanks to some divine intervention, broke a skate lace during her routine and finished well back.

Cabbie, take me to the finish line

Rosie Ruiz was the first woman to cross the finish line at the 1980 Boston Marathon.

No one knew who she was. A few people noticed she didn't seem quite as sweaty or as tired as some of the runners who followed her.

But she was crowned the winner.

The next day officials began reviewing tapes of the marathon. Funny thing, Ruiz didn't appear in any of the pictures, at least not until right before the finish line.

Race officials figured Ruiz had jumped on the subway or hitched a ride near the start of the race and rejoined it right near the finish line.

They stripped Ruiz of her title.

Cheating in ancient Greek

The ancient poet Pindar wrote about athletes in ancient Greece who were renowned for cheating.

Olympic organizers would erect statues paid for by cheaters as a warning to other athletes, who would have to walk past them on their way to the competition.

And in modern Greek

The first modern Olympics were held in Athens in 1896. Local hero Spiridon Louis won the marathon and the fans couldn't believe their good fortune when Greek runners also came in second and third.

They shouldn't have believed it. The fourth-place finisher ran over to the judges and told them he'd seen the guy who finished third ride half the race in the back of an ox cart.

They "lost" the Series

Sometimes people cheat in order to lose.

The 1919 Chicago White Sox were the best team in baseball and were expected to win the World Series against Cincinnati.

But they were also one of the lowest-paid teams in baseball. So when Chicago gangster Arnold Rothstein approached them with an offer of thousands of dollars each if they threw the World Series, eight of them said "yes."

The Sox lost the series in eight games, and a number of sports reporters thought something was a bit fishy and started writing about it.

Some of the players eventually confessed and a trial was set.

Miraculously, once the case went to trial those confessions disappeared. Without that evidence the players were aquitted. But it still ended their careers. They were banned from baseball for life.

Throwing the ball

For years, pitchers have been accused of scuffing balls. It allows them to give the balls an unnatural spin, which makes them harder to hit.

Rick Honeycutt was once kicked out of a game after the umps found a thumbtack taped to the inside of his glove.

He'd actually forgotten he'd put it there. At one point in the game, he used his glove to wipe the sweat off his face and cut a gash across his forehead.

I guess that would be called "scuffing the brain."

God scores for Argentina

Argentina and England met in
the 1986 World Cup of soccer.

There was no score until
Diego Maradona leaped in the
air near the England net and
knocked the ball in.

England immediately said
he'd hit the ball with his hand,
but the refs said "no."

Replays showed him
punching the ball.

After the game, Maradona
slyly avoided a direct answer when asked about the play.
He said perhaps it was the "Hand of God."

WEIRD FINISHES

We'll end the tour at the end, with some of the weirdest finishes in history.

You've probably dreamed of ending the big game with a basket at the buzzer, or a goal in overtime.

Reality isn't always like that.

Horses whinny, but you need a jockey to win

Seven horses lined up for the start of the St. Raymond Novices' Chase in Southwell, England.

With jockeys on them.

But one by one, all the jockeys fell off!

Tony McCoy was one of the first to fall. He got thrown as his horse went over one of a series of hurdles. McCoy figured that was it for the race so he started walking back to the change room.

He was almost there when he took a look back at the racetrack. He watched as one jockey fell off, then another, then another.

McCoy figured he had nothing to lose by trying to finish the race.

So he made his way back to the track, jumped back on his horse and won the race.

Zut, zut, zut et zut

French golfer Jean Van de Velde had a three-shot lead heading to the final hole of the 1999 British Open, one of the biggest events of the year.

It's very difficult to blow a three-shot lead. But Van de Velde hit his second shot into the grandstands around the green.

His third shot went in the water.

It took him two more shots to get the ball in the hole.

That left him in a tie for the lead, so they went to a playoff. But Van de Velde was French toast by then. Scotsman Paul Lawrie won the Open title.

Upset by Upset

One horse race has come to symbolize odd sports finishes for all time.

Around the early part of the last century there was one horse that was considered absolutely unbeatable.

His name was Man O'War.

By August 13, 1919, he remained unbeaten. So nobody expected him to lose on this fine afternoon at the Saratoga racetrack.

But as the race started, Man O'War was well back. Another, unheralded horse was in the lead and wasn't slowing down.

Man O'War tried and tried to gain the lead, but as they approached the finish line, Man O'War was second!

The crowd was stunned. The odds against this other horse winning were 100–1.

The winning horse's name was Upset.

Man O'War was obviously upset as well. He met Upset again a week later and won easily. Upset never won a race that big again.

Man O'War never lost again.

But that one loss remains a part of sports legend.

Ever since, when there's a surprise victory in sports, we call it an upset.

Hey! Get your butt outta my tuba!

The strangest finish, by far, was in the annual football game between Cal State and Stanford.

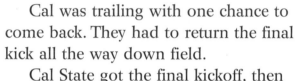

Cal was trailing with one chance to come back. They had to return the final kick all the way down field.

Cal State got the final kickoff, then avoided Stanford's tacklers by handing off the ball five times. The final runner even had to crash through Stanford's marching band to get into the end zone.

The band had assumed the game was over and poured onto the field.

It took a few minutes for officials to decide that Cal had indeed scored the winning touchdown.